JAMAICA

AF767581

PEP

Social Studies

Performance Task

GRADE 5

Practice Papers

hachette LEARNING

The Publishers would like to thank the following for permission to reproduce copyright material.

Photo credits

t = top, b = below, l = left, r = right, c = centre, b/g = background

p.7: (l) © Rido/stock.adobe.com, (r) © Rido/stock.adobe.com; p.8: (l) © gamelover/stock.adobe.com, (r) © Govind/stock.adobe.com; p.11: © max_776/stock.adobe.com; p.15: © max_776/stock.adobe.com; p.30: (l) © cdkproductions/stock.adobe.com, (r) © VIS Fine Arts/stock.adobe.com; p.36: (l) © Daniel Ernst/stock.adobe.com, (r) © Allistair/peopleimages.com/stock.adobe.com; p.49: © kotoffei/stock.adobe.com; p.51: (l) © Saint Images/stock.adobe.com, (r) © Saint Images/stock.adobe.com; p.52: © sonha/stock.adobe.com; p.57: © VectorMine/stock.adobe.com; p.60: (t) © blueringmedia/stock.adobe.com, (b) © BlueRingMedia/Shutterstock.com; p.62: © Pixsooz/stock.adobe.com; p.65: (t) © Rudzhan/stock.adobe.com, (b) © Svetlana/stock.adobe.com; p.67: © VectorMine/stock.adobe.com; p.78: © Albert Ziganshin/stock.adobe.com; p.79: (t) © Tryfonov/stock.adobe.com, (b) © Tverdokhlib/stock.adobe.com; p.81: © Iryna/stock.adobe.com; p.82: © Arid Ocean/stock.adobe.com.

Acknowledgements

Although every effort has been made to ensure that website addresses are correct at time of going to press, Hachette Learning cannot be held responsible for the content of any website mentioned in this book. It is sometimes possible to find a relocated web page by typing in the address of the home page for a website in the URL window of your browser.

Hachette UK's policy is to use papers that are natural, renewable and recyclable products and made from wood grown in well-managed forests and other controlled sources. The logging and manufacturing processes are expected to conform to the environmental regulations of the country of origin.

To order, please visit www.HachetteLearning.com or contact Customer Service at education@hachette.co.uk / +44 (0)1235 827827.

ISBN: 9781036005238

© Hodder & Stoughton Limited 2026

First published in 2026 by Hachette Learning (a trading division of Hodder & Stoughton Limited),
An Hachette UK Company
Carmelite House
50 Victoria Embankment
London EC4Y 0DZ

www.HachetteLearning.com

The authorised representative in the EEA is Hachette Ireland, 8 Castlecourt Centre, Dublin 15, D15 XTP3, Ireland (email: info@hbgi.ie)

Impression number 10 9 8 7 6 5 4 3 2 1

Year 2030 2029 2028 2027 2026

All rights reserved. Apart from any use permitted under UK copyright law, no part of this publication may be reproduced or transmitted in any form or by any means, electronic or mechanical, including photocopying and recording, or held within any information storage and retrieval system, without permission in writing from the publisher or under licence from the Copyright Licensing Agency Limited. Further details of such licences (for reprographic reproduction) may be obtained from the Copyright Licensing Agency Limited, www.cla.co.uk

Cover photo © GoodStudio-stock.adobe.com

Illustrations by Hyphen S.A./Konstantina Kyratzidou

Typeset by Hyphen S.A.

Printed and Bound in Great Britain by Bell & Bain Ltd, Glasgow

A catalogue record for this title is available from the British Library.

FSC www.fsc.org
MIX
Paper | Supporting responsible forestry
FSC™ C104740

Contents

How to use this book

Welcome to your PEP Practice Paper Book for Social Studies. For **Practice paper 1** we have provided some guidance on how to complete the work and given you sample answers. This will help you when you do **Practice papers 2** to **10**.

You are going to work through **Practice paper 1** with your teacher. This will help you to:

- Read questions carefully and decide the best answer to give.
- Learn how to get good results even if your answer is not completely correct.
- Understand what the different ratings mean and how you can improve your rating.
- Reflect on your own work to help you see what you did well and what you can improve on the next task.

Each task in this book has three supporting features.

Before you start …

This section helps you think carefully about questions and what it is you are being asked to do. Before you begin a test, read through the whole test carefully.

- Look at the words that are used in instructions. They give you clues about what you need to do and how much information you need to give.
- Here are some examples of instruction words you will find in the practice papers.

Analyse	Design	Find	Interpret	Say what
Choose	Draw	Find evidence	Investigate	What is
Compare	Explain why	How can you?	Justify	Work out
Decide	Fill in	Identify	Match	

- There are different levels of questions in each paper. Each paper starts with easy, recall questions and then ends with a more complicated task which requires you to think a little deeper.

Hints

These are given in the task itself to help you think about the questions and how you should answer them. As you progress, there will be fewer hints in the tasks.

Reflection

This section encourages you to think about your own learning and how you can improve on it.

Practice paper 1 also has a section called **How do you know how well you did?**
In this section, you can see how other students answered the questions and what rating they were given. The aim of this section is to show you what you need to do to get the best possible results.

Practice paper 1

This task has 3 parts:

- Part 1 has questions 1 and 2.
- Part 2 has questions 3 and 4.
- Part 3 has question 5.

Always check that you have everything you need before you start.

→ Before you start ...

When you do a performance task, it is useful to read through the questions first so you have an idea of what you will need to do. Start by skim reading all the questions.

The following task words and phrases appear in the performance task. Use them to complete the sentences.

label	write	draw	report	fill in	circle

i Read the text and then ________ the missing words.

ii Draw a ________ around the correct answer.

iii Write a ________ on what you found out, making sure you present the information in a logical way.

iv ________ a diagram to show the different parts.

v When you are designing your poster, decide on a picture to ________.

vi Use the space below to ________ your answer. Remember to check your punctuation.

Who are we?

You are a researcher working for a company that helps people trace their family tree. You are going to find out about different people in Jamaica and where their ancestors came from. Then you are going to write a report with the title, "Out of many, one people".

Part 1

All about ancestors

Question 1

Read the conversation between Jada and Daniel.

My grandmother always says that we are descendants of the original people of Jamaica – the Tainos. She says our ancestors lived in the mountains around the time the Spaniards arrived in 1494. The Tainos grew crops like cassava and sweet potatoes, and caught fish as well as shellfish. Granny says they taught the Maroons traditional cooking methods.

That is so cool. We are descendants of enslaved Ashanti people who were brought here in slave ships from Ghana, in West Africa in the 1500s. My dad says our ancestors were forced to work on the sugar plantations, owned first by the Spaniards and later by the British when they captured Jamaica in 1655. My great-great-great, I do not know how many greats, grandfather worked in the fields and his wife worked in the Great House, doing the cooking. He says Africans brought yams and cassava to Jamaica.

Look at the photographs and the conversation between the characters and use the information to complete the table.

a Fill in this table with information from Jada and Daniel.

	Jada's family	Daniel's family
Which ethnic group are their ancestors from originally?		
When did they arrive in Jamaica?		
What did they do?		
What food did they bring to Jamaica?		

b What do you know about the Maroons?

"Explain" means to give details. What would you mention to someone who has never heard about the Maroons?

- Explain who the Maroons were.
- Write **three** words or phrases which describe the kind of people the Maroons were.
- Identify **two** areas of Jamaican culture and state **one** thing that the Maroons contributed to each.

Descriptive words or phrases reveal traits or features. What are some of the traits associated with the Maroons?

Think of some of the categories used to describe a culture.

Question 2

Now read about what Kai and Shamana have to say.

My ancestors are Chinese. They came here in 1850, looking for a better life. At first, they had a contract to work on plantations, but this kind of life did not suit them and when their contracts finished, they opened shops and restaurants. Chinese food is the best! My parents still have a restaurant today.

Some of our story is the same. My ancestors also came here to work on the plantations just after Emancipation in 1834. They were indentured workers and they worked on the plantations for five to ten years. When their contracts were over, the government gave them land. Later they opened shops – many people of Indian descent still have shops today. We brought spices and curries to Jamaica.

a Fill in what you learned from Kai and Shamama.

	Kai's family	Shamana's family
Which ethnic group are their ancestors from originally?		
When did they arrive in Jamaica?		
What did they do?		
What food did they bring to Jamaica?		

"Emancipation" is another word for freedom.

b Shamana mentioned, "Emancipation in 1834". Explain what she means.

Remember the meaning of "explain".

This is asking you to explain why emancipation in 1834 is still important to Jamaicans today.

- State who was emancipated and by whom.
- What did the people need freedom from?
- Explain **three** things that happened to the emancipated people after emancipation.
- What were the options for the people who were emancipated?
- Why do you think Jamaicans celebrate Emancipation Day every year?

Part 2

Making a timeline and constructing a route chart

Question 3

Read through all the texts in Part 1 again. Then make a timeline showing the arrival of the different peoples in Jamaica.

Look back at what each character said in Part 1. What are the dates associated with each group of people?

You could draw it below, or you could use a tablet or computer to create your timeline using PowerPoint, Google Slides, or Canva.

ICT: Digital tools

Question 4

Read the names of places carefully before drawing and labelling the routes.

Look at this map of the world. Using different colours or different kinds of lines, draw in these routes. Label each route.

a slaves coming from West Africa to Jamaica

b Chinese workers coming from China to Jamaica

c workers coming from India to Jamaica

d trade going from Jamaica to Britain and Spain

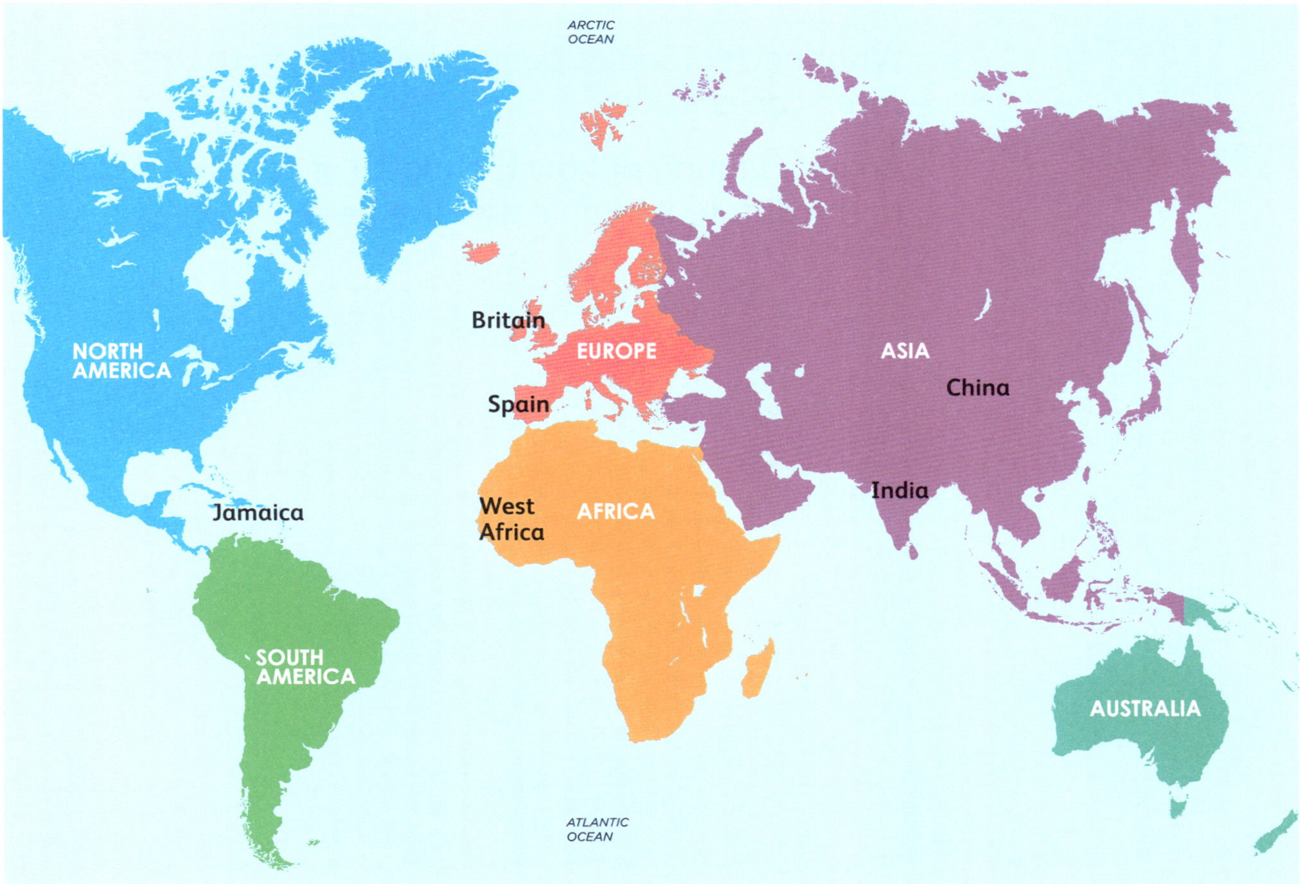

e Use an atlas or Google Maps to find the distance between Jamaica and one of the places on the map (such as China, West Africa or Britain). Write down the distance in kilometres. ______

Geography: Digital maps to explore migration routes

Mathematics: Distance between countries

ICT: Google Maps to search and compare routes

Part 3

Writing an essay

Question 5a

Plan your essay before you begin writing and use transition words or phrases to move from one paragraph to the next.

Now use all the information from the different sources and some of your own knowledge too to write an essay about the different peoples of Jamaica. The title of your essay is, "Out of many, one people".

When you write your essay, be sure to include:

- How and when the different groups of people arrived in Jamaica.
- What each group of people contributed to the Jamaican culture.
- An explanation of how the motto of Jamaica relates to the different people who live here.

Question 5b

Using your essay, record a short 2-minute documentary or podcast episode using a phone or tablet.

ICT: Creating with digital tools

Practice Paper 1 Self-evaluation

How do you know how well you did?

Now that you have worked through the task, you are going to look at some answers that students gave to see how they were rated. Then you can rate your own answers using this scale.

1 Beginning	2 Developing	3 Proficient	4 Highly proficient
Answers show no evidence or very little evidence that the student understands the concepts.	Answers show some evidence that the student partly understands the concepts.	Answers show that the student is competent and understands most of the concepts.	Answers show that the student understands all the concepts very well and may have found the task quite easy.

We will look at some of the answers to the four different levels of questions.

Recalling information

Questions 1 and 2

These are simple questions, asking you to read, find information and fill in a table.

Question 1a: Here you fill in the table, based on information from Jada and Daniel.

	Jada's family	Daniel's family
Which ethnic group are their ancestors from originally?	Tainos	Ashanti slaves from Ghana
When did they arrive in Jamaica?	descendants of original people of Jamaica	1500s
What did they do?	raised chickens and grew vegetables	worked on sugar plantations
What food did they bring to Jamaica?	jerk chicken	yams and cassava

Question 1b: Here you give your own answer, based on what you know. For example:

The Maroons were local people who lived in the mountains of Jamaica. Many escaped slaves joined the Maroons. The Maroons were fierce fighters against the occupying nations. They contributed jerk chicken to Jamaican culture and dances like the dinki minki.

Question 2a: Here you fill in the table, based on information from Kai and Shamana.

	Kai's family	Shamana's family
Which ethnic group are their ancestors from originally?	China	India
When did they arrive in Jamaica?	1850	just after Emancipation in 1834 or earlier
What did they do?	first contract to work on plantations, then shopkeepers	first indentured workers on plantations, then shopkeepers
What food did they bring to Jamaica?	Chinese food	spices and curries

Question 2b: Here you give your own answer, based on what you know. For example:

The Emancipation in 1834 is when the slaves were set free. The slaves were African people and they were set free by the British, who ruled Jamaica at that time. After emancipation, some slaves became farmers and some slaves stayed on the plantations. Some ran away to the mountains to join the Maroons.

Skills and concepts

Question 3

This question requires you to think a little deeper. You need to apply your **skills and concepts** to construct a timeline.

- 1400s Tainos live in Jamaica
- 1500s Ashanti slaves arrive from Ghana
- 1830s Indian indentured workers arrive
- 1834 Emancipation
- 1850s Chinese workers arrive

Strategic thinking

Question 4

This question is a mix of **using your concepts** and **thinking strategically** to plot routes on a map.

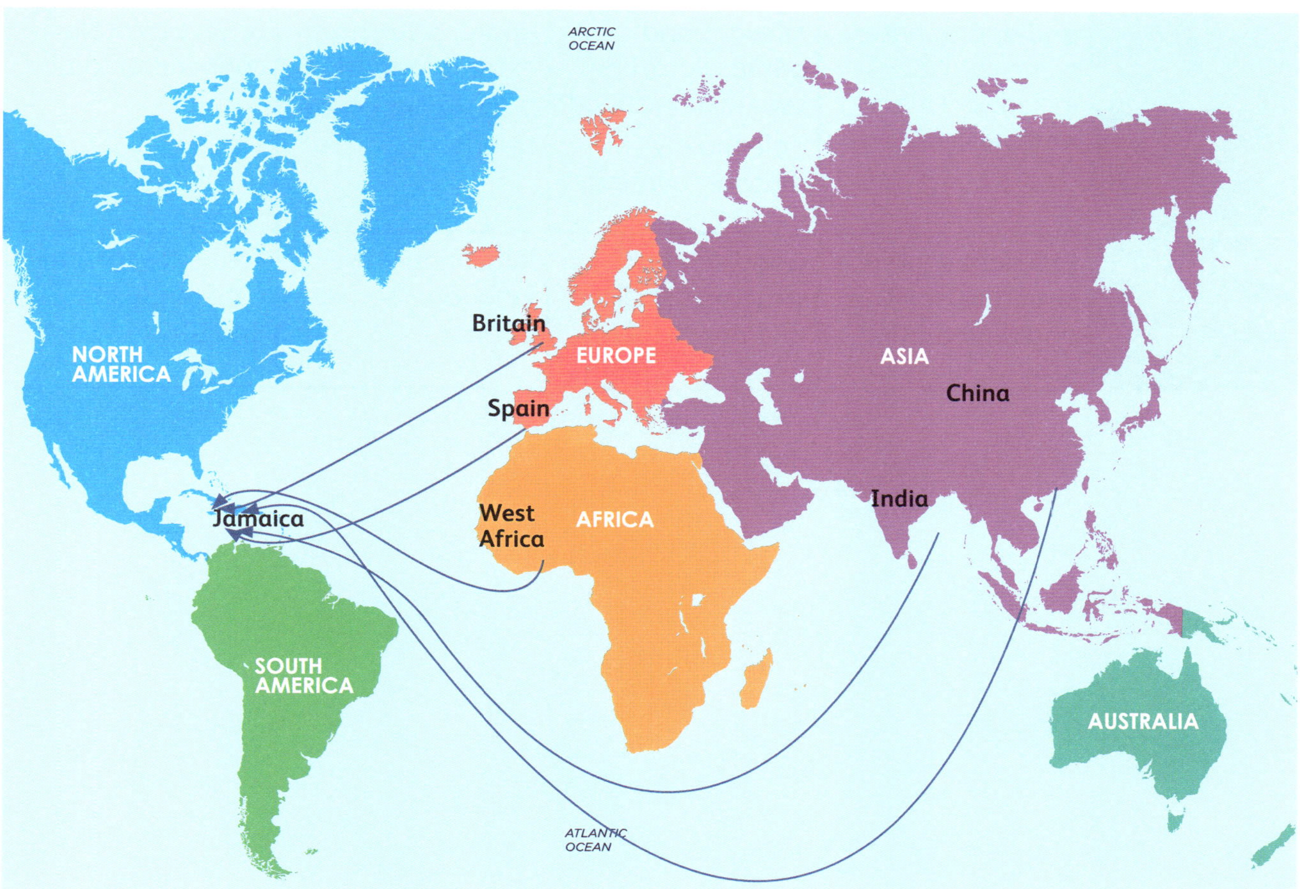

Extended thinking

Question 5

This question asks you to synthesise all the information you have from the sources and write an essay. You cannot just give a simple right answer, you have to think carefully about how to structure your report.

This rubric shows how a reviewer would score the task.

Essay *Out of many, one people*	4 Highly proficient 5	3 Proficient 3–4	2 Developing 3–2	1 Beginner 2–1
Planning	Planning is evident – four well-constructed paragraphs.	Ideas are in separate paragraphs.	Some confusion in structuring and ordering information.	Not well planned.
Content	Content is relevant and appropriate; some own ideas included. Title matches content.	Content is fairly relevant and appropriate; one own idea included. Title mainly matches content.	Content is appropriate, no extra information. Vague connection to title.	Content is lacking or very thin. No connection to title.
Language use	Excellent sentence structure, spelling and punctuation.	Good sentence structure, spelling and punctuation.	Reasonable use of language, some errors.	Struggles to write coherently in English.

Reflection

Complete this flow chart.

My strengths

____

____

____

Evidence of my strengths

____

____

____

My goals for the next performance task

____

____

____

My plan to reach the goals

____

____

____

Practice paper 2

This task has 3 parts:

- Part 1 has questions 1 and 2.
- Part 2 has question 3.
- Part 3 has question 4.

Answer all the questions.

Famous people and places

You have been asked to tell visiting students from another country about some of our famous people and places.

→ Before you start ...

- Read each source carefully.
- What kind of information is each source giving? Is it fact or opinion?
- Underline the main sentence in each paragraph. The rest of the sentences support that main sentence. This will help you with your answers.

Part 1

Our heroes and heroine

Question 1

You want to begin by introducing your guests to the country's only heroine and to marronage.

SOURCE 1

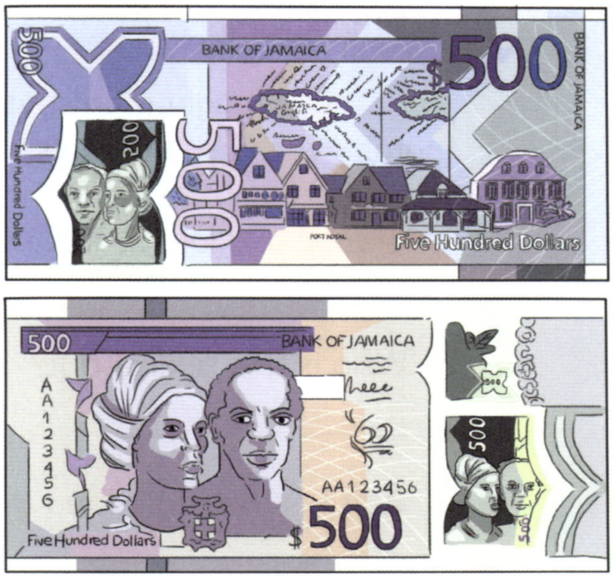

a Who are the two people on this Jamaican banknote?

b Why are they on the banknote, in your opinion?

c Can you name **four** other famous people that are on Jamaican banknotes?

d Why is National Heroes Day significant for Jamaicans?

SOURCE 2

__________ is one of our national heroines. She founded Nanny Town in the Blue Mountains in the 1720s with her brother, Quao. The town is situated deep in the mountains on a ridge which made it very easy to defend from attackers. __________ and her followers used an *abeng* to call their warriors.

__________ fought many battles against the British – most notably the First Maroon War from 1728 to 1729. She led many successful raids on the plantations, and helped slaves to escape and join with the Windward Maroons.

a Who is this text about?

____

Sometimes the main idea is implied, not stated.

b What is the main idea in the first paragraph?

____

____

A supporting idea gives more information about the main idea.

c Write down **two** supporting ideas from the first paragraph.

____

____

d What is the main idea in the second paragraph?

____

____

e Write down **two** supporting ideas from the second paragraph.

____

____

f What else do you know about this famous person? Write down **two** facts that you know.

Question 2

SOURCE 3

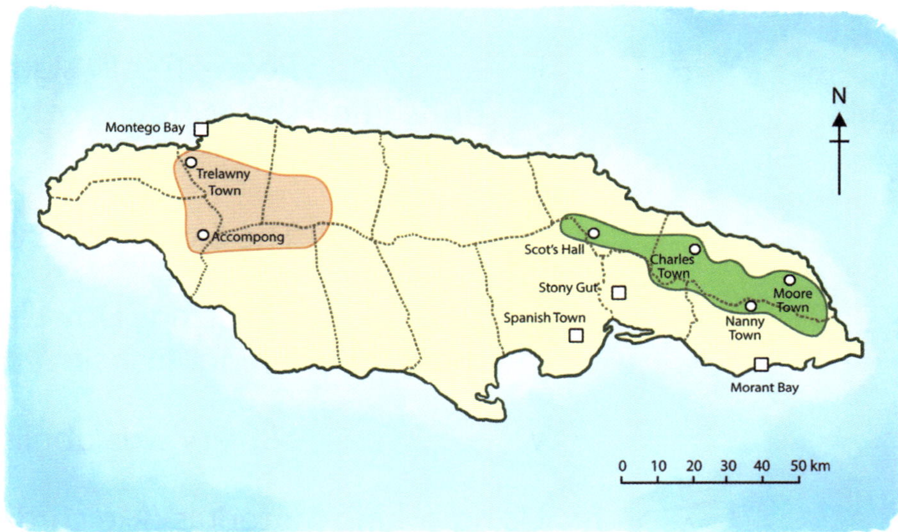

a Briefly describe the Maroons to your guests.

b Mark on the map where the Trelawny Maroons settled and where the Windward Maroons settled.

c Mark a cross on the map to show where Sam Sharpe was born and died.

d Circle the correct answer:

(A) Sam Sharpe was a Baptist preacher who led a rebellion.

(B) Sam Sharpe was a slave who wanted a better life.

(C) Sam Sharpe was a farmer on a plantation in the west.

e Fill in the gaps to say when the two famous people on the banknote fought for the rights of Jamaicans.

i ____________ – ____________: The Maroon Wars.

ii ____________: Peace Treaty signed between the British and the Maroons after years of violent struggle.

iii ____________: The Slave Trade was abolished.

iv ____________: Christmas Day Uprising, the largest mass rebellion against slavery.

v ____________: Slavery was abolished.

f Using simple materials (like cardboard or paper), create a model of Nanny Town, showing its mountain location and defences.

Technology: Physical models

History: Maroon resistance or plantation life

Geography: Landforms and how they shape human activity

Part 2

Describing our National heroes and heroine

Question 3

a Draw lines to match the description to the famous person.

Sam Sharpe	was the leader of the Morant Bay rebellion in 1865.
George William Gordon	said, in 1832, "I would rather die on yonder gallows than live in slavery."
Paul Bogle	was a great warrior, but also a spiritual leader of the Jamaican people.
Nanny of the Maroons	was a landowner and an attorney who tried to help people by buying land for them and getting their goods to the market.

b Read these two verses from the Jamaican National Heroes Song and, using your own knowledge, circle the correct answers.

George William Gordon, far seeing statesman
struggled for human rights and dignity
he was unjustly executed
for raising his voice against oppression

Chorus:
Forward, forever united
Students, workers and farmers

Paul Bogle of Stony Gut
fought against oppression and deception
leader, preacher and martyr
He died in the cause of justice

i Paul Bogle and George William Gordon were active:

(A) before Emancipation.

(B) after Emancipation.

ii George William Gordan was falsely accused of being part of the Morant Bay Rebellion.

(A) true

(B) false

iii Paul Bogle:

(A) marched 72 miles from Stony Gut to Spanish Town to talk to the governor.

(B) marched 72 miles from Spanish Town to Stony Gut to talk to the governor.

c Describe, in your own words, what the chorus of the song means to you.

____

____

____

d Design a creative element, such as a digital slide with facts or hero quotes.

ICT: Creating with digital tools

Part 3

Synthesising what you know

Question 4

It is time for your guests to leave Jamaica and you want them to have memorabilia of their visit, so you designed a scroll with information about some of the people on the other bank notes.

On your scroll, write **one** paragraph each about **two** people other than the ones in Source 1 that are on Jamaica's bank notes.

Each paragraph should reveal:

- The name and details of why that person is considered an important figure in Jamaica.
- An explanation of what that person contributed to the development of the nation.

Remember to use transitions within your paragraphs.

Reflection

Once you have checked your answers to the task, complete these statements about your work.

- I now know ______.
- I need to know more about ______.
- These things went well ______.
- I could do better if I ______.
- In my next task, I will pay attention to ______.

Practice paper 3

This task has 3 parts:

- Part 1 has questions 1 and 2.
- Part 2 has questions 3 and 4.
- Part 3 has question 5.

Remember to read all the questions carefully and to answer all the questions.

Beautiful Jamaica!

You work for the Jamaican Tourist Board and you have been asked to design a brochure for tourists, giving them some information on Jamaica's culture, including music, carnival, food and dance. To start, you will do some research and then decide on four aspects to write about in your brochure.

→ Before you start …

When you do a task or test, you can answer the questions in any order. It is better to do the questions that are easy first. That way you have more time to spend on the more challenging parts of the task.

This task has **five** questions.

Skim through the questions and decide on an order to answer them.

Write your order here:

- First, I will do question ________.
- Next, I will do question ________.
- Then, I will do question ________.
- After that, I will try question ________.
- Lastly, I will finish question ________.

Part 1

Studying sources

Question 1

Read the different sources and then answer the questions.

SOURCE 1

Maypole dancing

Maypole dancing is a popular cultural and traditional dance still found in Jamaica. The maypole dance originated in Europe where people danced around the pole with ribbons on the first of May each year to celebrate the harvest and the fertility of the land.

Up to sixteen dancers take part. Each dancer holds the end of a ribbon and the dancers move in and out in a pattern so that the ribbons get wrapped around the pole. Popular patterns are the grand chain, basket weave and candy stripes.

Maypole dancing is usually done to mento music. In some cases, reggae music is used to give the dances a modern touch.

SOURCE 2

The quadrille

The quadrille is a ballroom dance for four couples which was brought to Jamaica by plantation owners in the time of slavery.

There are two styles of quadrille: ballroom and camp style. The camp style was inspired by the slaves and it is more Creole in nature. It is popular in rural areas. Both styles have elements of African dance, including fancy footwork, bent knees, throw-back actions and hip movements. The music for a quadrille is normally supplied by a live mento band.

When you compare, you look for similarities; when you contrast, you look for differences.

a Complete this table to summarise the sources and compare and contrast maypole dancing with quadrille dancing.

	Maypole dancing	Quadrille dancing
Origins		
Number of dancers		
Dance movements or steps		
Music		

b What is your favourite kind of dancing? Write **four** sentences about it, giving the same information as the information given in the table.

Origin

Number of dancers

Dance movements or steps

Music

Question 2

Read this article about Carnival and then answer the questions.

"Pre-determined" means that the route is arranged before the festival.

IT IS CARNIVAL TIME!

Carnival, or Bacchanal Jamaica, is famous all over the world. It is celebrated during the Easter week, and many famous local and international soca/calypso and reggae artists perform. The event is celebrated in towns including Negril, Mandeville, Montego Bay and Ocho Rios, with each area organising a costumed street parade, blow-out fêtes and, of course, Las Lap – the final jump-up before the end of Carnival.

Kingston is the main focus. People converge here for the children and adult's costumed parade. The Adult Road Parade marks the climax of the festival. It follows a pre-determined route through Kingston to Emancipation Park in Oxford Road where the best bands are judged for the Band of the Year title.

a Where is Carnival held?

______

b When is it celebrated?

______

c What route does the Adult Road Parade follow in Kingston?

______

d You need to help tourists understand Jamaican language. Write definitions for these words from the article.

i Soca/calypso: ______

ii Reggae: ______

iii Blow-out fêtes: ______

iv Las Lap: ______

v Jump-up: ______

Part 2

Finding information

Question 3

Look at a map of Jamaica showing parishes and their capitals.

Are there national buildings, historical monuments or beautiful places to visit?

a Write down the name of your parish and its capital.

____

b What would tourists come to your parish to see?

____

____

Mining, tourism, farming or fishing?

c What is the main industry in your parish?

____

Use the scale to work out the distance.

d Roughly how far away is the capital from where you live?

____

Question 4

Time to get tasty! What food is Jamaica famous for? Study the photographs and answer the questions.

a Name the two dishes in the picture.

____

"Represents" means symbolises.

b Which dish do you think most represents Jamaica? Explain why.

____

____

c Imagine you are building a solar-powered food cart. List three items your cart would need to work and explain how using solar power helps the environment.

Technology: Function of a food cart

Science: Solar energy, sustainability

Part 3

Synthesising what you know

Question 5

Now it is time to put your brochure together. You need to choose **four** aspects of Jamaican culture. Divide your page into quarters. Put one amazing aspect of Jamaican culture in each quarter.

Remember!

- This brochure is for tourists – you want them to come and visit Jamaica.
- Give your brochure a big, bold, beautiful title.
- Then, give each quarter of your brochure an amazing and interesting title.
- Add photographs or sketches to illustrate your brochure.
- Use bold letters and colour if you have coloured pens.

Reflection

Go back through your own answers to the questions in this task.

- Which ones did you do well?

- What made these ones easy for you?

- Which ones did you struggle with?

- What made them difficult for you?

- What two things can you do to make these types of questions easier for yourself in the future?

Practice paper 4

This task has 2 parts:

- Part 1 has questions 1 and 2.
- Part 2 has question 3.

Answer all the questions and remember to read all the instructions carefully.

Hellshire beach, where have you gone?

The residents of Hellshire are very worried about the way the erosion of the beach has affected their livelihoods. They want to put together a list of suggestions for the parish council:

- to prevent further erosion
- to help them to keep earning a living.

→ Before you start ...

- Read through all the sources carefully.
- Underline all the facts in one colour and the opinions in another. This will help you with your answers.

Part 1

Study the sources

Question 1

Read through all the sources about the erosion of Hellshire beach. Then answer the questions.

SOURCE 1

Hellshire beach, where have you gone?

Staff reporter
June 2023

Hellshire beach was one of the most popular tourist beaches in Jamaica, famous for its white sands and seafood. But much has changed since 1968 when it used to be a Sunday beach area for families to come and picnic and swim.

Now the beach has eroded to almost nothing. The water comes right up to the buildings and many vendors have been forced to relocate their shops. Residents have tried to hold the water back by using stones and tyres, but to no avail.

The National Environment Planning Agency (NEPA) is working to reduce the soil erosion, but with climate change, sea levels are rising and the shoreline is being eroded further every year. This is not helped by higher sea temperatures and the more intense hurricanes that the Caribbean is experiencing.

SOURCE 2

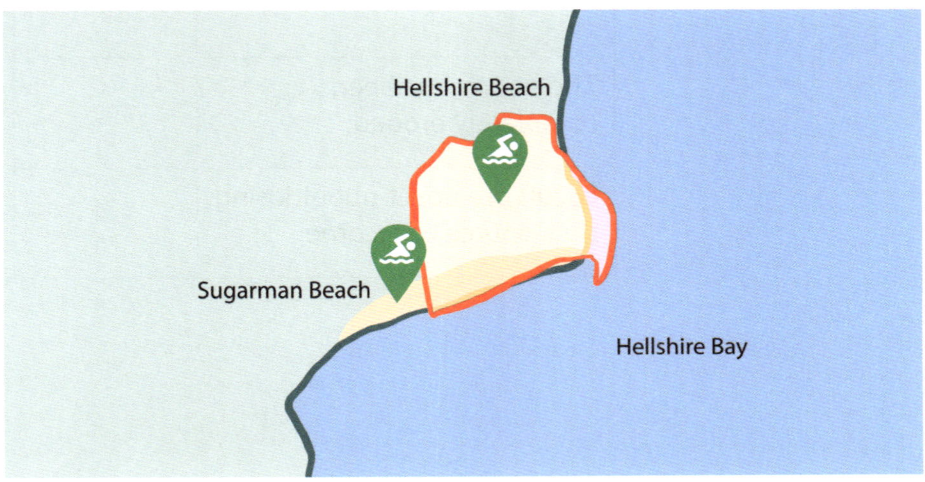

SOURCE 3

The waters reach so high now we do not even have places to tie our boats. The beach is completely gone. It is a disaster. The parish council must do something.

Tourists used to come to my restaurant, it was very famous. Families would come to the beach every Sunday and then come up and eat lunch in the middle of the day. Now there is no beach and no reason for the families to come. Some tourists come to see the change and say it's a crying shame. I may have to close down. The parish council must do something.

The main point is the central idea of the text.

a What is the main point of Source 1?

____

____

b Tick ✔ which of these statements is supported in the sources.

	Source 1	Source 2	Source 3
Hellshire Beach was famous.			
The beach has been completely eroded.			
Locals are upset about losing their source of income.			

Question 2

Refer to the map of Jamaica and your own knowledge to answer these questions.

a In which parish is Hellshire Beach?

b What is the capital of that parish?

c Which of these emblems represent the parish?

d Give the absolute co-ordinates of Hellshire beach.

e Using the scale, calculate the distance between the capital of this parish and Kingston as the crow flies.

"As the crow flies" means in a straight line, so you measure the distance between the capitals directly.

f Explain what a parish council is.

g What kind of things would the parish council of this parish be responsible for? Give at least **three** examples.

Part 2

Putting it all together

Question 3

When you give a suggestion, first present the problem, then your solution. Remember to write in polite English.

As a concerned citizen of the community, you have volunteered to write a letter, which includes a list of suggestions for the parish council. When you write your letter, be sure to include:

- at least **three** suggestions for preventing further erosion
- **three** suggestions for helping people (like fishermen and restaurant owners) to keep earning a living.

Question 4

You have been asked to design a simple barrier or structure to help protect Hellshire Beach from erosion. List three materials you would use and explain why they are a good choice.

Science: Environmental changes and erosion

Geography: Coastal features and human impact

Design & Technology: Protective structures

Reflection

There are **three** questions in this paper.

Use this scale to rank the questions in order from the one you found easiest to the one you found most challenging.

Easiest	→				Most challenging

Complete these sentences.

- I found question ________ easiest because ____________________.
- I think question ________ was challenging for me because ____________________.

Practice paper 5

This task has 3 parts:

- Part 1 has questions 1 and 2.
- Part 2 has question 3.
- Part 3 has question 4.

→ Before you start ...

Make sure you have everything you need. Read each question carefully before you answer it.

Parish councils

You are going to research parishes and parish councils (municipal corporations) in Jamaica. You will find out what each parish produces and what the councils do before writing a report on your own parish council. In your report, you will:

- explain how the council is structured
- say what it does
- give **two** examples of where you think your parish council could help the citizens of your parish.

Part 1

Using what you know

Question 1

Look at the map of Jamaica, showing the different parishes.

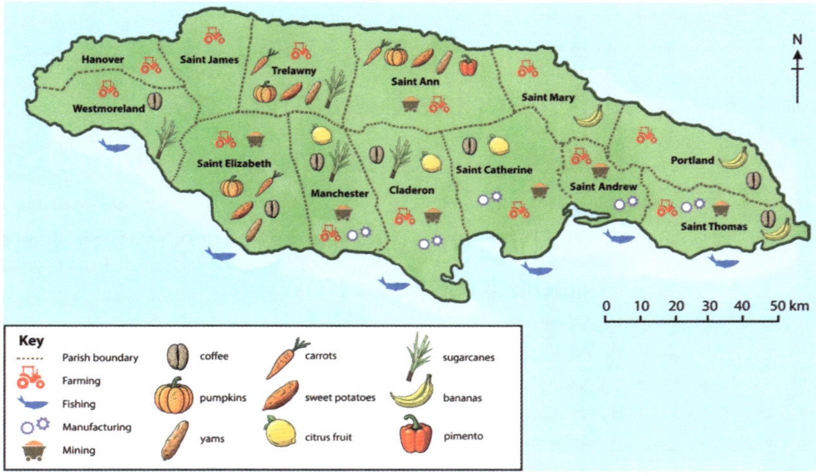

a Complete this table by writing in the name of the parish next to its capital.

Parish	Capital
	May Pen
	Lucea
	Kingston
	Mandeville
	Port Antonio
	Half Way Tree
	Saint Ann's Bay
	Spanish Town
	Black River
	Montego Bay
	Port Maria
	Morant Bay
	Falmouth
	Savannah-la Mar

There are three counties in Jamaica.

b Shade in the counties on the map and add the labels to the map.

It produces the most food.

c Which parish is known as the breadbasket?

____

d Write down the parishes that rely on fishing for their income.

____

e Underline the correct answer.

Coffee is grown in the wetlands / in the mountains.

f What the weather is like in the **three** parishes where bananas are grown?

(A) hot and wet

(B) cold and dry

(C) hot and dry

(D) cold and wet

Question 2

Now answer some questions about your own parish.

a What is the name of your parish and its capital?

____

"import" means bring into an area from another place; "export" means sending products from where they are made or grown to another place.

b What are the main industries and products in your parish?

i industry: _______________

ii products: _______________

c What products does your parish export?

____

d What products does your parish import?

____

For example – at the market, at a shop, at a supermarket, from a vendor.

e Where does your family buy:

i vegetables: ______________________

ii fish: ______________________

iii meat: ______________________

iv made objects, like pots and pans:

____

Mining, tourism, a monument (give its name), a festival, etc.

f What is your parish known for?

____

____

Part 2

Parish councils and their work

Question 3

Read this extract from a textbook and then answer the questions.

> Parish councils (municipal corporations) are in charge of a parish. There are two arms of the councils. The administrative arm remains unchanged when there is an election and consists of the secretaries and administrators who run the office. The political arm, on the other hand, consists of councillors who are elected by the people. New councillors are appointed each time there is an election. These councillors appoint a mayor.
>
> Each councillor is responsible for a particular area in a parish. Councillors put together committees to help them do their jobs.
>
> Some of the duties of a councillor and their committees include roads and works, finance, environment, disaster relief, poor relief, public health and sanitation and commercial services.
>
> Property taxes are used to pay for these responsibilities. At least 30% of all property taxes go to fund community services like garbage collection, streetlights, water supply, sanitation and trading licences.

Read the text again. Who do you think should be at the top?

a Make a flow chart showing how a municipal corporation is structured.

b What is the correct form of address for the person at the top of your flow chart in Question 3a?

(A) Sir

(B) Your worship

(C) Mrs/Mr Mayor

(D) Boss

Think about the following: Do potholes need to be repaired? Should there be more/fewer vendors? Do you need traffic lights or a stop street? Is there too much garbage? Are there areas that are unsafe for children? Is there erosion that needs fixing?

c Think carefully about your local parish council and your parish. What are **two** areas of your parish where you think there could be some improvement? Use a flow chart to make notes.

Parish Council

Area for improvement 1

Area for improvement 2

Part 3

Writing a report

Question 4

Now it is time to write your report. In your report, you should:

- explain how your municipal corporation is structured
- outline what it does
- give **two** examples of where you think your parish council could help the citizens of your parish.

Give your report a title.

You could use headings in your report.

Present your points with numbers or bullets.

Make sure you give good reasons for the changes you think your parish should make.

Reflection

Give yourself some personal feedback about your work on this task. Use these sentence stems as starters.

- I am already quite good at
  ______________________________.
- I can get better at
  ______________________________.
- This is what I can do to improve
  ______________________________.

Practice paper 6

This task has 3 parts:

- Part 1 has questions 1 and 2.
- Part 2 has questions 3 and 4.
- Part 3 has question 5.

Always check that you have everything you need before you start. Answer all the questions in each part in the spaces provided.

→ Before you start …

- Underline the key words in each question. These are clues that tell you what you need to do.
- Highlight any important information that is given in the question. You might need to use this to find the answer.

Rain and shine

You are a climate and weather expert tasked with studying the weather and climate of Jamaica, as well as its effects on the landscape. Your goal is to provide valuable advice. You advise farmers in your area on:

- weather predictions
- ways of planting that will reduce erosion.

Part 1

Reading the weather

Question 1

Read the weather chart and answer the questions.

Monday	Tuesday	Wednesday	Thursday	Friday	Saturday	Sunday
cloudy	cloud/sun	thunder	thunder	rain	sun	sun
21 °C	25 °C	24 °C	24 °C	23 °C	28 °C	27 °C

a What is the weather like on the weekend?

b Describe how the weather will change from Monday to Friday.

c What is the difference between the highest and the lowest temperature?

d What would you wear on Friday that you might not wear on Saturday?

e Design a weather outfit for a rainy day and another for a sunny day. Label the materials your outfit needs and explain why they're good for each type of weather.

Science: Weather patterns and temperature

Technology: Clothing design for weather protection

Question 2

"In detail" is another way of asking for more information.

a Describe, in detail, the weather where you are today.

____

____

b Use this chart to record what the weather in your area was like in the past five days. Estimate the temperatures and draw in your own weather symbols.

d What is the climate like in Jamaica? Choose from these words and underline your answer.

(A) polar

(B) tropical

(C) Mediterranean

(D) temperate

e Explain your answer to Question 2d by describing the general weather patterns in Jamaica.

____

____

Part 2 Collecting data from charts and photographs

Question 3

Look at the two drawings of different kinds of rainfall.

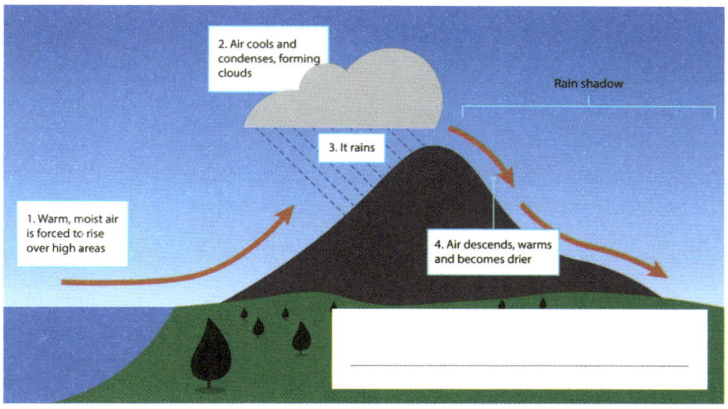

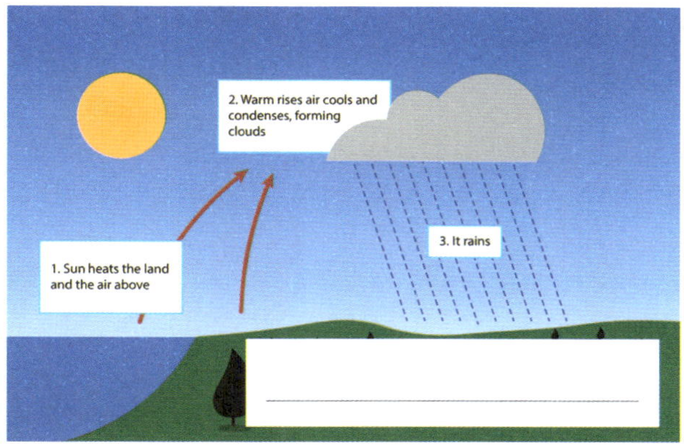

a Label the drawings: which shows convectional rainfall and which shows relief rainfall?

b Describe convectional rainfall by putting these sentences in order 1–6.

☐ and as it rises, it forms clouds

☐ that they shed their moisture as rain

☐ water evaporates from dams and rivers

☐ the warm rising air is full of water vapour,

☐ on a hot day,

☐ the clouds become so heavy,

c Label the relief rainfall diagram by matching these sentences to A, B, C and D.

☐ i Air descends and becomes warm and drier.

☐ ii Air cools and condenses, forming clouds.

☐ iii Warm moist air is forced to rise over high areas.

☐ iv It rains.

d Name two areas in Jamaica that experience relief rainfall. Refer to a map to help you.

Question 4

Study this photograph.

a How do you think the deep gullies formed here?

b What is the name of the horizontal method of planting crops shown in the photo?

Consider the direction that water flows on a slope.

c What would have happened if the farmer had planted their crops in rows facing downwards?

Part 3

Analysing and interpreting data

Question 5

Create a brochure about weather patterns and planting to avoid soil erosion that farmers could quickly read. When you write the text for your brochure, be sure to include:

- when it rains
- how much it rains
- what crops are grown in your area
- how much water they need
- what to do if there is too much/too little water
- what to do to make the soil healthy.

Give your work a title.

You could use headings in your report.

Present your points with numbers or bullets.

Make sure you give good reasons for the advice you are giving.

Reflection

- What did you find difficult or confusing about this task?
- What extra information would have been useful?
- How can you find this extra information?

Practice paper 7

This task has 3 parts:

- Part 1 has questions 1, 2 and 3.
- Part 2 has question 4.
- Part 3 has question 5.

Answer all the questions.

→ Before you start …

- Skim read all the questions.
- Circle or highlight any instruction words.

Hurricane season!

It is hurricane season. You decide to read up about hurricanes so that you can write a useful pamphlet for people in your parish to help them prepare themselves for a hurricane.

Part 1

Using context clues to answer questions

Question 1

Read the sources carefully and then answer the questions.

SOURCE 1

Hurricane Gilbert, in 1988, is still one of the most destructive hurricanes that has hit Jamaica in the last hundred years. It produced a 5.8 m storm surge and brought so much rain to the mountainous regions that it cased flash flooding.

49 people died and thousands were left homeless – the roofs were literally blown off their houses. Some people had to be rescued from mudslides.

There were millions of dollars of damage – destroyed crops, buildings, houses, roads and power lines. Schools and businesses had to close and it took many months before life returned to almost normal.

SOURCE 2

Most intense landfalling Atlantic hurricanes
Intensity is measrued solely by central pressure

Rank	Hurricane	Season	Landfall pressure
1	Labor Day	1935	892 mbar (hPa)
2	Camille	1969	900 mbar (hPa)
2	Gilbert	1988	900 mbar (hPa)
4	Dean	2007	905 mbar (hPa)
5	Cuba	1924	910 mbar (hPa)
5	Dorian	2019	910 mbar (hPa)
7	Janet	1955	914 mbar (hPa)
7	Irma	2017	914 mbar (hPa)
10	Cuba	1932	918 mbar (hPa)
10	Michael	2018	919 mbar (hPa)

SOURCE 3

HURRICANE FORMATION

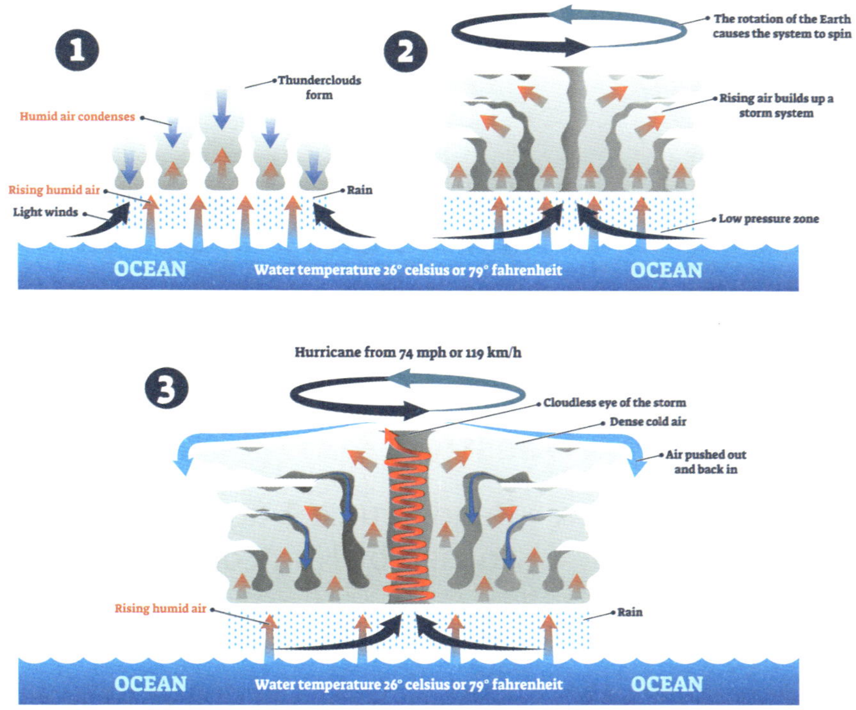

a What is the main point of each source?

Source 1: ______________________

Source 2: ______________________

Source 3: ______________________

b Tick ✔ which of these statements is supported in each source.

	Source 1	Source 2	Source 3
Hurricanes happen in Jamaica.			
Hurricane Gilbert was one of the most destructive.			
Hurricanes are moved by large, rising air currents.			

c Write down **three** facts from the sources and say which source they come from.

d Write down **one** opinion from the sources and say which source it comes from.

Question 2

a Read Source 1 again. Make a list of all the damage caused by Hurricane Gilbert.

b Read Source 2 again. How many hurricanes were there in the 1900s?

c How many hurricanes have there been in the 2000s so far?

d What does this tell you about the rate at which hurricanes are occurring?

You will need to come to your own conclusions about the rate at which hurricanes are occurring.

Question 3

a Using the diagram in Source 3, write an explanation of how a hurricane occurs. You should have at least **five** points.

Part 2

Interpreting drawings

Question 4

Look at the pictures of a mangrove swamp.

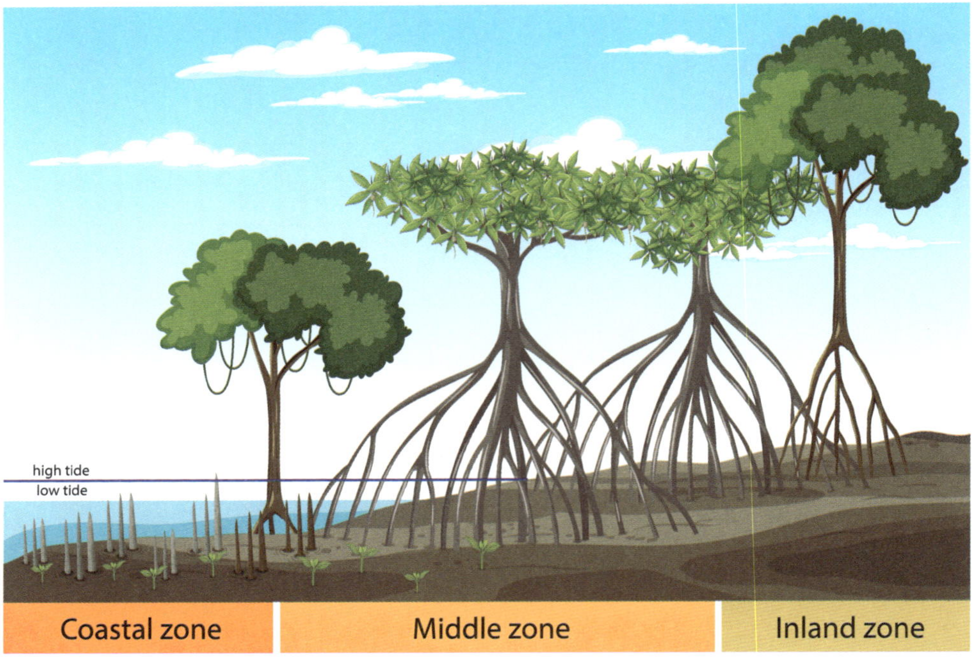

a What are **two** functions of the roots of a mangrove?

b Explain how a mangrove swamp can help to reduce a storm surge.

c Refer to the second picture. What other uses does a mangrove swamp have?

Think about the functions of the mangroves and how they can be destroyed by human activity.

d What can we do to protect mangrove swamps?

e Design a simple model to show how mangrove roots stop waves or trap soil. You can sketch it or build it using sticks, paper or recycled items.

Science: How mangrove roots protect the coastline and support wildlife

Geography: Coastal zones and how human activity affects natural habitats

Design & Technology: Models

Part 3

Creating a useful list

Question 5

Here is a partly completed list of what you need to have in your hurricane kit.

a Use this source as a starting point. Complete a list of everything a person would need in a hurricane kit.

b Create a pamphlet that will be emailed to the people in your community at the start of hurricane season.

When you create your pamphlet be sure to include:

- two threats posed by hurricanes
- an explanation of why people need to prepare for hurricanes
- an action plan with **six points** of what people need to do to prepare for a hurricane.

Reflection

- Make a list of **three** things in this paper that you did well.
- What could you do better?
- Write down **one** thing that you learned in another task that helped you here.

Practice paper 8

This task has 2 parts:

- Part 1 has questions 1, 2 and 3.
- Part 2 has question 4.

Always check that you have everything you need before you start. Answer all the questions in each part in the spaces provided.

→ Before you start ...

- Read through all the questions.
- Underline the question words (where, how, what etc.).
- Think about how you can answer each question.

Forests and wetlands

You are investigating forests and wetlands. Your mission is to write a letter to the mayor of your parish about how people can help to keep these natural areas beautiful, safe and unpolluted.

Part 1 Investigating forests and wetlands

Question 1

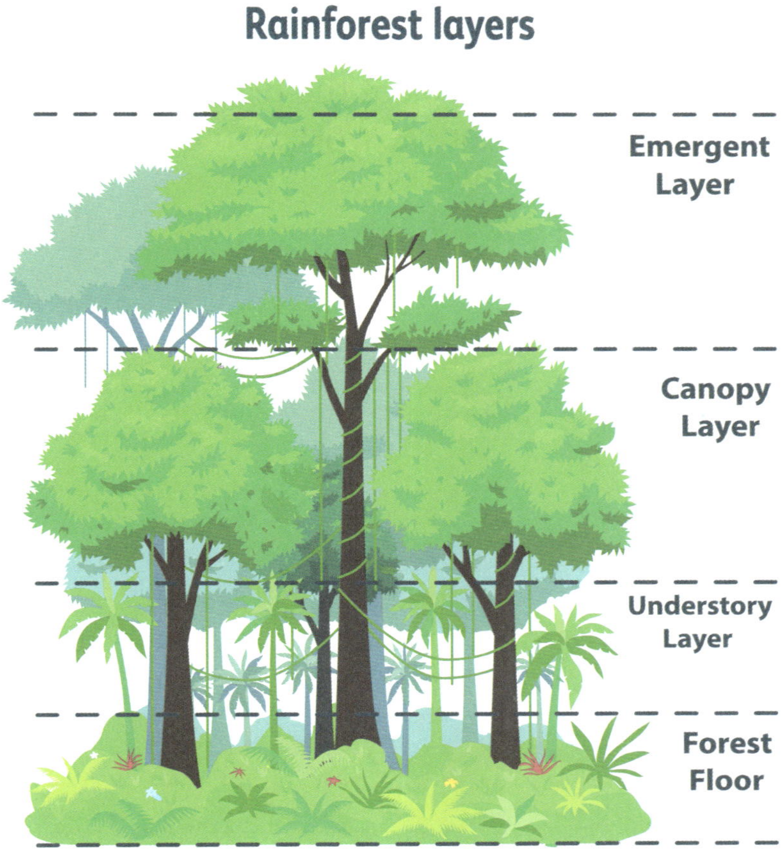

a Where are most of the forests in Jamaica?

b What kinds of forest do you find in Jamaica?

Use these words in your paragraph: tallest trees, sunlight, shade, compete.

c Look at the picture and the diagram on the previous page. Write a short paragraph explaining how a forest works.

Think about who lives there and about the function of these layers.

d What would happen if you cut down the emergent and canopy layers in a forest?

e What would happen if you cleared out the understory and forest floor layer?

Brainstorm this with your friend if you are running out of ideas.

f Why are forests useful to humans and animals? Write at least **five** reasons.

Question 2

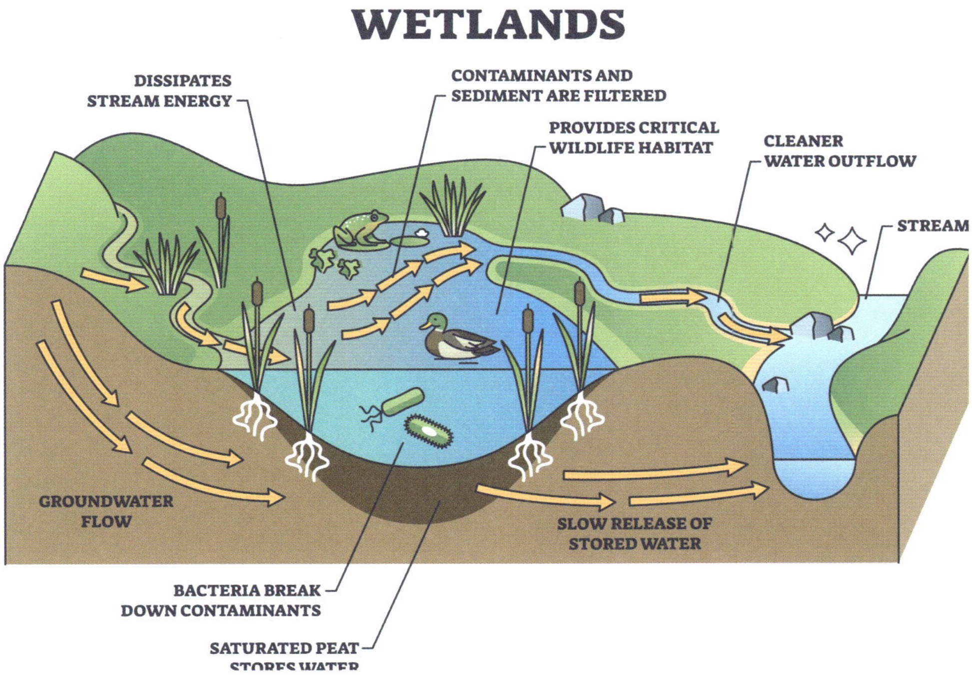

a What **two** things happen to harmful contaminants in a wetland?

b What kinds of birds and animals live in a wetland?

c Draw a simple wetland food chain, showing a producer, herbivore and carnivore.

d Use the picture on the previous page to explain, in point form, why wetlands are essential to people and animals.

____

____

____

____

____

Question 3

Read this article carefully and then answer the questions. Underline words you do not understand and then look them up in your dictionary.

Jamaica was once almost entirely covered by forest, but today more than 75 per cent of the lowlands forest has been cut down. The land was cleared for agriculture. The forest that is left is in the remote mountain regions.

This deforestation meant that when Hurricane Gilbert hit Jamaica in 1988, there were big mud slides and land slippage, because there was no vegetation to hold the soil in place.

Gilbert is not the only one to blame though. The fast-growing agricultural industry has meant that many acres of land were cleared for coffee and other crops. And then there is bauxite mining – this is actually the largest cause of deforestation in Jamaica. Bauxite is extracted by open cast mining, which means complete removal of the vegetation and the topsoil. A problem is also the roads built into the forests, because once those access roads are cut, it opens the way for charcoal burners, loggers and yam stick traders to move in.

When the trees go, rivers and streams dry up, and plants and animals die out.

a How much forest remains in Jamaica?

b Why was the forest cut down in the beginning?

c What is the largest cause of deforestation in Jamaica?

d Explain what *open cast mining* is. How is it different from mining for gold, for example?

e Who else uses the access roads into the forest?

Question 4

Use two trays or containers. Fill both with soil.

- In one tray, place leaves or small sticks on top to act as forest cover.
- In the other, leave the soil bare.

Gently pour water over both trays.

What do you observe? Which soil stays in place better?

Science: Plant layers in forests; erosion and water filtration

Geography: Types of forests and wetlands in Jamaica

Part 2

Synthesising what you know

Question 5

You are going to write a letter to the mayor of your parish about either:

- keeping wetlands unpolluted or
- looking after forests and reasons why this is necessary.

When you write your letter, be sure to include:

- an explanation that gives **two** functions of wetlands or forests to Jamaica's ecosystem
- an explanation of **two** things that the mayor and parish council can implement to preserve either the wetlands or the forests.

Remember to use the correct form of the letter and to address the mayor correctly.

Reflection

Think about any questions or parts of questions that you got wrong.

- Did you understand the question and know what to do? If not, what can you do about this?
- Did you use information incorrectly? If so, what can you do to avoid these mistakes in future?

Practice paper 9

This task consists of 2 parts:

- Part 1 has questions 1 and 2.
- Part 2 has question 3.

Make sure you answer all the questions. Remember that you can answer them in any order. It is better to do the questions that are easy for you first. That way you have more time to spend on the more challenging parts of the task.

→ Before you start ...

- Read through the task carefully.
- Mark all the positive comments about mining in one colour and all the negative comments in another to help you.
- Read carefully before you decide which way you are going to argue: for or against.

Polluted flows

You are taking part in a debate at school about bauxite mining in Jamaica.

- You need to decide whether you are for or against bauxite mining.
- In preparation, you will read some sources and then draw up a list of pros and cons. You will use your list to write up your argument.

Part 1

Reading and answering

Question 1

Read the article and then answer the questions.

SOURCE 1

The river, once a vital resource for domestic use and livelihoods, has become a symbol of contamination and despair.

A resident of the community since April 1980, Mr Brown, unveils a chilling revelation. Since the bauxite mine opened, whenever it rains, waste is said to emerge from the bauxite plant, causing the fish to die and the river to become contaminated. He explains how the river's once-pure waters are now contaminated. The people of the village depend on this river for their very survival. In a place with limited employment opportunities, "this has affected us all and made life hard."

a How is the bauxite mine polluting the river?

____

____

b How long has the pollution been going on for?

____

c How long has Mr Brown been a resident in the community?

____

d What has Mr Brown noticed that happens when it rains heavily?

____

____

Question 2

Now read these two sources carefully and answer the questions.

SOURCE 2

Bauxite is a mineral found in limestone rock. It is mined in the open-cast method, then transported to kilns where it is dried and crushed. The crushed bauxite is mixed with water, caustic soda and lime to create a liquid or slurry. The alumina is extracted from this solution and the slurry is dumped into red mud lakes. Alumina is used to make aluminium and it is also a part of cement and many other products like abrasives and glass.

SOURCE 3

Jobs for Jamaicans! Work for our people!

New Bauxite Quarry requires:

- shift supervisor
- 3 foremen
- 200 bauxite miners

Please enquire, with your CV, showing relevant experience at jobs@JamaicaBauxite.com.

a Say what kind of sources 2 and 3 are.

____

____

b Which source gives purely factual information?

____

c Which source has some persuasive language in it? Write down examples of **two** phrases.

____

____

d What positive things do these two sources say about bauxite mining?

e Underline the positive things about bauxite mining in the two sources.

Part 2

Building an argument

Question 3

a Now look back over the three sources and your underlining, and fill in these columns.

Negative things about bauxite mining	Positive things about bauxite mining

b Now decide whether you are going to argue for or against bauxite mining.

Write your argument here.

When you write your arguments, be sure to include:

- the position you have taken on bauxite mining
- an explanation that gives **three** reasons bauxite mining is positive or negative for Jamaica.

Reflection

- What did you find easy about this task?
- What was difficult?
- Did underlining the two different positions in different colours help you?

Practice paper 10

This task has 3 parts:

- Part 1 has questions 1 and 2.
- Part 2 has questions 3 and 4.
- Part 3 has question 5.

Always check that you have everything you need before you start. Make sure you answer all the questions.

→ Before you start …

- Read the whole paper carefully.
- Underline all the instruction words, so you know what you have to do.

Space Invaders!

You are Zog, the alien in your spaceship.

This task has 3 parts:

- Your leader has told you to investigate the Universe and find a good place to land your spacecraft.
- You need to find a planet that supports life, where people are friendly and will welcome you.
- And, on that planet, you need to find the perfect place to land.

Part 1

Investigating the Universe

Question 1

As you travel the Universe in your spaceship, you notice a very interesting system.

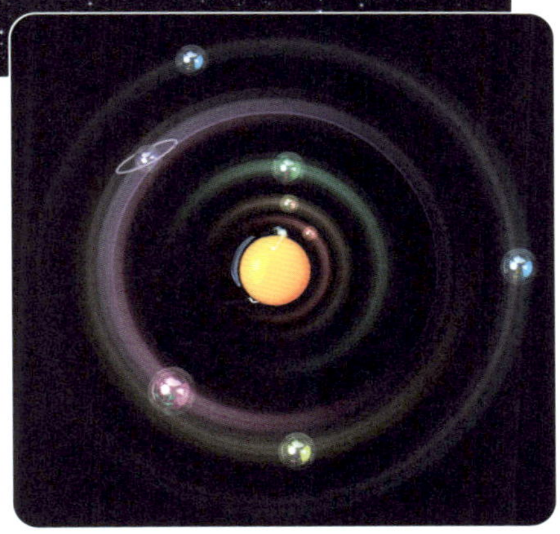

Report back to your leader.

"Centre" means middle.

a What is at the centre of this system?

____

Look closely at the illustration of the system. Can you spot any clues that help you identify its name?

b What is this system called?

____

c Use the names below to label the planets on the illustration.

Earth	Jupiter	Mars	Mercury	Neptune
Saturn	Uranus	Venus		

Think about what you need to live as a being who lives on this planet.

Question 2

Which planet in this system will support life?

- Name the planet.
- Explain where it is situated in the system.
- Give at least **three** reasons to support your answer.

Question 3

Imagine you have a spaceship that needs to land on a new planet and you have to make a life-support pod! List three systems your life-support pod will need (such as air, water and food) and explain how they help keep astronauts alive.

Science: Planets in the solar system; conditions needed to support life.

Technology: Space habitats

Part 2

Giving the co-ordinates

Question 3

As you circle the Earth in your spaceship, you see a group of islands.

Report back to your leader.

> How do you decide if the group of islands is in the northern or southern hemisphere?

a Tell her if this group of islands is in the northern or southern hemisphere.

____

b The island you like best is Jamaica. Which islands are to the north, west and east of Jamaica?

____

____

c Tell your leader the nearest line of latitude.

____

d Give the **two** nearest lines of longitude.

____

e Now give her the absolute co-ordinates for the island called Jamaica.

____

Question 4

As you get closer to the beautiful island of Jamaica, you must decide where to land.

What land features does this type of map show?

Look carefully at the map before writing the labels.

a What are the brown and green areas on the island that you see from Space?

---

b Match these labels to the places on the map. Write them on the map.

- Kingston
- Montego Bay
- Dry Harbour Mountains
- Blue Mountains
- Wetlands
- The Palisadoes

c Your ship can land on water or on land. Where do you think is the best place to land?

____

Think about ease of landing, safety, the surface on which you land and the closeness to people.

d Give **three** good reasons for your answer to Question 4c.

____

____

____

____

Think about the meaning of the motto and use it to guide your answer.

e The motto of Jamaicans is "Out of many, one people". Do you think they will welcome you? Say why or why not.

____

____

____

Part 3

Writing a report

Question 5

Now using what you have discovered, write a report for your leader, explaining the following:

- which planet you have chosen and why
- which island you have chosen and why
- where you should land and why
- how you think the people of Jamaica will receive you and why.

Reflection

- Did you enjoy this Practice paper? Explain why or why not.

- What did you find easy to do?

- What was challenging?

- What do you need to revise, in order to do better next time?